THE UNITED STATES
VIRGIN ISLANDS

A PHOTOGRAPHIC PORTRAIT

First published in the United States of America by:

Twin Lights Publishers, Inc.
10 Hale Street
Rockport, Massachusetts 01966
Telephone: (978) 546-7398
http://www.twinlightspub.com

ISBN 1-885435-40-1

10 9 8 7 6 5 4 3

Book design by
SYP Design & Production, Inc.
http://www.sypdesign.com

Printed in China

Other titles in the Photographic Portrait series:

Cape Ann
Kittery to the Kennebunks
The Mystic Coast, Stonington to New London
The White Mountains
Boston's South Shore
Upper Cape Cod
The Rhode Island Coast
Greater Newburyport
Portsmouth and Coastal New Hampshire
Naples, Florida
Sarasota, Florida
The British Virgin Islands
Portland, Maine
Mid and Lower Cape Cod
The Berkshires
Boston
Camden, Maine
Sanibel and Captiva Islands
San Diego's North County Coast
Newport Beach, California
Phoenix and the Valley of the Sun
Wasatch Mountains, Utah
The Florida Keys
Miami and South Beach, Florida
Maryland's Eastern Shore
Asheville, North Carolina
Charleston, South Carolina
Savannah, Georgia
Southeastern Arizona

CONTENTS

ST.JOHN 6

54

ST.CROIX

ST.THOMAS 90

Ask people on St. John about Steve Simonsen and they usually reply, "He's the best photographer on the island." Short of a visit by Ansel Adams—unlikely since he's dead—or David Doubilet—who does drop by occasionally—that assessment is true. But don't take my word for it. Open the pages of this beautiful book and see for yourself.

Steve makes his living photographing the US Virgin Islands. The man is not only gifted at what he does, he loves it and breathes it and has been doing so for more than 20 years. As might be expected, such a confluence of ability and intense application has produced remarkable results, a distillation of which you hold in your hands.

Admittedly, he is blessed with wonderful material—the radiant seas that bathe our shores, golden beaches underlining the emerald hills, darting iridescent wildlife in the air or under the sea, as well as the islands' people, with everything they have built.

While that wonderful material is available to all with eyes to see, it is Steve's particular talent that he sees to the heart of the archipelago and captures the quintessence of its beauty. The clarity of his focus and the colors of his work twine together in often breathtaking ways.

The US Virgins, formerly the Danish West Indies, had a tumultuous early history, with an economy based on violence—conquest, piracy, then sugar and slavery, and the explosive revolts of a proud people responding to oppression. But after slavery collapsed and the arrant fortune seekers left, the islands reverted into the hands of those who loved them, and their natural tranquility returned.

Left to their own devices, the people lived simply off the sea and the soil, sustained by a vibrant culture centered around God, family and friendship. In retrospect, those years were a Golden Age—marked not by money but by its absence. "Golden" referred to the Rule, not to a CEO's parachute.

Until recently the license plates here said "American Paradise." The convicts that made them may not have thought so, but plenty of others do; these islands attract all sorts of people, searching for their own dram of bliss.

Lovers come here to be married, on a beach at sunset, or on a bluff at sunrise, a few even underwater in scuba gear, and for one dramatic couple, naked on horseback in the surf at dawn.

Sailors flock here to charter boats and take advantage of the steady breezes, unremittingly good weather and abundance of safe anchorages. Families come here for safe swimming beaches and campgrounds, extended families come here for reunions and can pick from villas or cottages or hotels on beaches, atop mountains, in a National Park or downtown Charlotte Amalie.

The adventurous can parasail high above the sea, windsurf along its surface or dive the South Drop. Less physically daring types can explore restaurants or try the odds at a casino, while the unabashedly sedentary can sip Pina Coladas by the hotel pool while getting a foot massage. For everyone the lovely views, delicious air and warm encircling seas are a source of delight all year round.

And not just visitors...people from all over the world have made these islands their home. Indian merchants, Palestinian grocers, Vietnamese cooks, St. Lucian masons, Dominican fruit sellers. The early ferry to St. John bringing day laborers used to unload a flood of lively "patois" but now it's a wave of Spanish that pours down the dock. Struggling ashore at night in remote bays it used to be Haitians and Dominicans; now young Chinese appear at first light on the East End road, neatly dressed and eager to work.

The islands have always been a place where currents meet and jostle. Jutting headlands may accelerate the stream, deep bays may harbor backwaters, or the tide create eddies—and hurricanes may drive in disruptive seas from any direction—but in the end the turbulence subsides, the various currents mingle and all become part of the broad, deep westward flow, inexorably driven by the earth's slow turn.

(opposite)

On a calm, crystal clear day, the kind we get when a norther is approaching, every detail of Hurricane Hole and the East End Peninsula can be made out from afar. Beyond them lie Pelican, Norman and Peter in the British Virgins. And beyond them—Africa.

ST. JOHN

(previous page)

Hurricane Hole

Hurricane Hole has been beloved by sailors for five centuries, because its landlocked "creeks," offer almost bullet proof protection from stormy weather. In good weather the few boats anchored there feel like they are up a river, surrounded by green. When a hurricane threatens, the holes fill up with boats and their lights at night resemble a town.

(above)

Trunk Bay

Lying in the soft surf, you feel the coarse clean sand gently wash back and forth across your skin—a full body loofa—while light plays in the clouds and in the foam on a beach.

(opposite)

Century Plant

Each year the century plant refrains from blooming, but bides its time for decades. Then, one day in April, it begins its climactic bloom, sending forth a stalk 20 feet high, with outspread branches covered by masses of tiny flowers, thousands upon thousands which slowly turn from delicate new born green to a bold yellow that stands out with a shout against a backdrop of blue sky or water. At the peak of its glory it begins to die, slowly fading, hardening, turning into a statue of itself—which the locals use half a year later for island Christmas trees.

(left)

View from Bordeaux Mountain

Driving from Cruz Bay to Coral Bay you round a ridge high up on Bordeaux Mountain, and suddenly one of the world's great views falls away below. Islands and coves, bights and peninsulas, beaches and promontories, deeps, rocks, reefs and shallows streaming with light are strewn out to the horizon. Some things never change...and others do. Thirty years ago there was but one boat moored in Coral Bay, a small wooden fishing skiff.

(below)

Haulover Bay

The isthmus at Haulover Bay connects the rugged East End peninsula with the rest of St. John. Before boat engines were available, railroad track ran across the isthmus and oxen hauled over heavily laden sloops to save them the arduous beat against adverse winds and seas when rounding East End.

(opposite)

Sailing Vessel Pepper

The sweet Pepper was built on St. John by a local shipwright to a design inspired by the traditional native sloops. She daysails out of the Maho Bay resort.

Diver and Dolphin

Recently, dolphins have been coming into anchorages and swimming around yachts with people, even giving one lucky girl a ride around the harbor. Maybe dolphins are becoming aware of the respect and love felt for them by the islands' sailing community.

Underwater Beauty
Nature was partial to the USVI when she added colorful under-water treasures to their already generous portion of beauty ashore.

(opposite)

Red Sea Grape Leaf and Palm Tree

*Sea grapes and palm trees line
the North Shore road where it
descends and runs along the
edge of Maho Bay while the
bottle green shallows beckon.*

(above)

Moravian Church, Coral Bay

*The grand old Emmaus Moravian
Church of Coral Bay is one of
the landmarks of the Virgin
Islands, noted for its unmatched
acoustics, its beautiful rafters and
its thick stone walls. The sanctuary also serves as the island's
finest concert hall and, in time of
need, as a hurricane shelter. A
Moravian church has stood on
this spot since 1789.*

(above)

Hawksbill Turtle

*Gliding beneath the waves, the
photographer's wife gets close
enough to study the intricate
golden markings that set off this
big hawksbill turtle's head and
flippers. These gentle, lovable
animals are generally tolerant of
divers, letting them approach—a
trait sometimes to their cost.*

(opposite)

**Kayaks near Mary Point in
The Fungi Passage**

*The Virgin Islands' many points
and bays are idyllic for the
sea-kayaking crowd. This group
is traveling past Mary's Point
through the Fungi Passage, an
area that makes mariners wary
of the strong currents.*

(above)

Great Cruz Bay

This aerial shot of the Westin Hotel at Great Cruz Bay shows this world class resort's famous pink structures, manicured grounds, and large pool. Right off the beach a fleet of boats swinging at their moorings gives the hotel guests an ever-changing mobile to watch.

(opposite)

Kids and the Sea

St John is a great place to raise children. The sea offers constant fun—healthy, invigorating, uplifting fun. The award winning KATS (Kids and the Sea) program in Coral Bay, staffed by dedicated volunteers, has been teaching the island's children to row, sail and race for 14 years.

(pages 20–21)

Privateer Point

This rugged, current wracked point marks the southwest entrance to the Sir Francis Drake Channel. In its lee is a wide bay, rolly but safe in normal weather.

Whistling Cay and Mary Point

Brilliant white water, white as the whitest snow, outlines the steep-to, bold coast of Whistling Cay and behind it, Mary's Point.

(top)

Concordia Eco Tents

The eco resort at Estate Concordia is built on a steep hillside, the units connected by attractive wooden walkways and steps.

(bottom)

View of Lamesur from Bordeaux

High up Bordeaux Mountain, at the very top of St. John, vibrant vegetation hems in the path and gnarled hardwoods shade it. A hiker looks far down the steep valley and sees Lamesur Bay, calling her off the mountain and into the sea.

(above)

Booby at French Cap Cay

The gimlet-eyed booby can swim underwater like a beaked bullet, powered by huge webbed feet, and strike faster than the eye can see. He spends his days flying and diving over and under clear blue seas. Whence the name "booby?" Because nesting pairs wouldn't desert their chicks to save themselves when men arrived. That says more about the men who named them than it does about boobies!

(opposite)

Sailing Vessel *Rusty Nail*

The USVI abounds with lovely anchorages—around a headland, behind a barrier reef, off an arc of glowing sand—one right after another. Just as you think you've found perfection there's a cove waiting a short sail away, that might be better yet.

**Moonrise off Nanny Point,
Privateer Point and Flanagan**

*When the moon is exactly full at
sunset, it rises above the horizon
just as the sun sinks below the
horizon. The best place to see
this is on the high seas, with
unobstructed horizon all about.*

Gone Ketchin'

*The popular sports fishing boat
"Gone Ketchin'" coming home at
sunset after a day of "fish'n"
out on the South Drop. There the
underwater mountain range,
whose peaks are the Virgin
Islands, suddenly drops away
to depths of two miles—choice
fishing waters. The VI almost
owns the world record for
blue marlin.*

(above)

The Salt Pond

This salt pond, just west of Drunk Bay, still makes fair quantities of salt in dry years. In the past, these ponds produced a cash crop. Before refrigeration, salt was used to preserve meat and fish and salt ponds played an important role in the West Indian economy.

(right)

Door at Dennis Bay

A heavy old island door at Dennis Bay is fitted with hurricane brackets so that it can be barred against storms or the night, then opened onto the kind of vista that has made the islands world famous.

(above)

Anchored at Twilight

Anchored in a snug cove as twilight comes is one of the quiet delights of cruising on St. John.

(opposite)

Snorkeler and Southern Stingray

This snorkeler is relating to an amiable stingray at Honeymoon Bay—but not feeding it. Though stingrays are among the friendliest animals in the sea—some as tame as dogs—feeding them is probably not a good idea.

Windspirit

The "Windspirit," one of the new breed of "sailing" cruise ships, frequently visits the Virgin Islands. The sails are more for looks than propulsion, but that's just fine with the passengers.

Driftwood

Who knows where this piece of driftwood started its voyage? Perhaps expelled by the Amazon River far to the south, or by the Gambia River across the Atlantic in Africa, here it came to rest at Cinnamon Bay in St. John.

(opposite)

Carnival

Carnival—farewell (vale) to the flesh (carne)—is celebrated just prior to Lent. An explosion of color, rhythm, and dance—i.e. life—before the coming of death, Carnival is part of a universal mythos, but is nowhere celebrated so exuberantly as in the Afro-Indies and Brazil.

(above)

Pale Moon Rising

A huge pale moon rises over Cruz Bay like a silent ghost peering over a ridge to see if it's time yet to make its debut.

Starstruck

Snorkelers at Leinster Bay examine a golden orange starfish before putting it back, right side up please, on the sand. Leinster Bay is the definitive place to find starfish

(left)

Island Brilliance

It is amazing and somehow reassuring that the island flowers so resemble the corals of the reef in form and brilliance. There is a pattern, above and below, and where there is a pattern there may be a purpose.

(below)

Turks Head Cactus

This Turks Head Cactus, so named for its fez-like cap, has a fruit ready to eat. It tastes like a cross between a strawberry and a star apple. These cactus flourish in dry rocky soil.

(opposite)

Happy Hour

It's happy hour for everyone! Especially for this bananaquit if it finds sugar in the glass that the canny photographer probably put there to get the shot. Island porches commonly put out bowls of sugar to attract these bright, lively little creatures, well out of the cat's reach, please.

(above)

Caneel Bay Resort

This is just one of several pristine beaches that ring the Caneel Bay Resort. In its heyday kings, presidents and movie stars came here to escape.

(opposite)

Sailboat at Trunk Bay

It is no secret that the best thing about going to sea is getting back to land. The sea scours and bleaches the senses like fasting or prison. It heightens the appreciation of life's ordinaries such as the first feel of sand between the toes. Sand—that soft/hard fringe of land's bulk rising from beach to cloud capped mountain, bearing on its back the multitude of quick warm life so intoxicating after days on the salt void.

(left)

Ruins

This aerial shot of St John's Annaberg makes the old planta-tion ruins look like a medieval fortress with a tower, set to guard a critical waterway. Which, in a way, is true since the best bone fishing flats on the island extend from the shore below into Leinster Bay.

(opposite, top)

Annaberg Plantation

Flame trees of summer frame the silvered stone walls of Annaberg Plantation.

(opposite, bottom)

Annaberg Ruins at Sunrise

The stone tower, standing proud against the fiery dawn, is a part of Annaberg, the scenic recon-structed sugar plantation above Leinster Bay. Bonefish flats extend along the coast here.

(above)

Evening at Mongoose Junction

This beautiful shopping complex was built like a cathedral, to last for centuries, conferring dignity and grace upon its portion of the island.

(opposite)

Overlook at Trunk Bay

At intervals along the North Shore road, stone walls mark an overlook where one's mind can be filled with an exquisite image—in this case Trunk Bay. Not so long ago, people traveling by land along St. John's north shore track had the choice of riding a horse or donkey, or walking. Today, despite a surfeit of vehicles, the scenery still inspires people to use their feet.

St. John Sunrise

*The Sun King flares across
the eastern sky, leaving fire
aloft, shadows below.*

Hawksnest Villa View

*The view from Hawksnest Villa
explains—better than words ever
could—why people are drawn
here, away from cities and snow.*

(left)

Spotfin Butterflyfish "Chastodan Ocellatus"

A pure, ethereal yellow ignites the fins of a demure spotfin butterflyfish as it swims out of a dark cave and into a ray of sunshine.

(below)

French Angelfish

Awsome and exquisite, like the gold tipped scales of a French Angelfish browsing on a shallow reef, an underwater realm magically appears when one dons a mask and slips below the surface of the warm sea.

Sailing into the Sunset

The Virgin Islands arguably offer the best sailing in the world, and every sort of boat can be found plying its protected waters. Here, a gaff rigged cutter sails into the golden glow of day's end.

Petroglyphs at Reef Bay

The pre-Colombian petroglyphs at Reef Bay were carved where they could reflect in the water at their base. This picture shows the eerie effect—spirits peering out of the pool.

Waterfall

This beautiful waterfall at Reef Bay feeds the pools of the petroglyphs. This picture was taken during a very rainy period because in normal dry weather the falls are just a trickle down the face of the rock.

Gibney Beach

Listed as Hawksnest on the charts, it is better known as Gibney Beach, after the family that has owned it for fifty years. Discouraged by The Bomb, The Gibney's considered it their get-away from a civilization bent on self destruction. Ironically, they sold a small piece of it to Robert Oppenheimer, who headed up the Manhattan Project.

(left)

Bougainvilleas

Every summer Bougainvillea emblazon the country roadsides with red bursts of happiness.

(opposite)

Hummingbird and Aloe Vera, Two icons of the Antilles

Aloe is found close to many island kitchens, where a piece of it can be immediately sliced off and applied to a burn with nearly miraculous results.

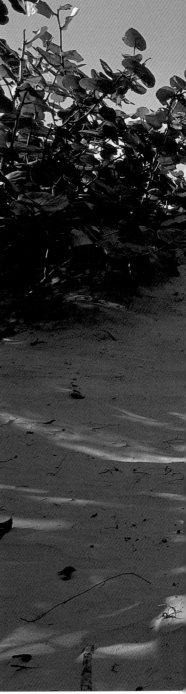

(top)

Tree Frog

Tree frogs are beloved for their sweet chirping at night, especially in the freshness following a swift passing rain squall.

(bottom)

Mongoose

The mongoose was initially imported to the West Indies to kill another European import—rats, which wreaked havoc on the local bird life. But instead, mongoose and rat opted to share the spoils. Rats, nocturnal, ruled at night, the mongoose reigned by day.

Cinnamon Bay

Sand and shadow, bordered by sea grape, leads on to the blue light of paradise—in this case Cinnamon Bay

ST. CROIX

(previous page)

St. Croix

Turquoise marks the narrow strip of shallows near the shore and beyond. Stretching indefinitely beyond the horizon lie the cobalt depths of the ocean, two miles deep between St. Croix and St. Thomas.

(above and opposite)

Snorklers at Buck Island Reef

The Buck Island reef is ancient, massive, convoluted and delicate. Catacombs deep within the reef house whole nations of fish. Old cities have fallen in upon themselves time and again, time out of mind, their bones and shards the foundation of new growth.

Buck Island National Monument

*It would be hard to find an island
more blessed by clean white sand
and incredible shades of water...
water like wet air, so clear and
pure one is tempted to deep
breathe it and return again to the
arms of "mother ocean."*

Sandy Point

Sandy Point is the extreme southwest tip of St. Croix. Seas from south, west and north curl around it, heaping up a lavish beach of bright sand. Here the gradual decline of the island into the sea creates a broad expanse of sandy shallows—nature's palette for mixing water and light into incendiary hues of aquamarine.

(opposite)

St. Croix's North Coast

The view of St. Croix's north coast from a height graphically illustrates the famous drop off that makes for such spectacular scuba diving.

(above)

Blackbarred Soldier Fish

A diver hovers like a shepherd over a school of blackbarred soldier fish.

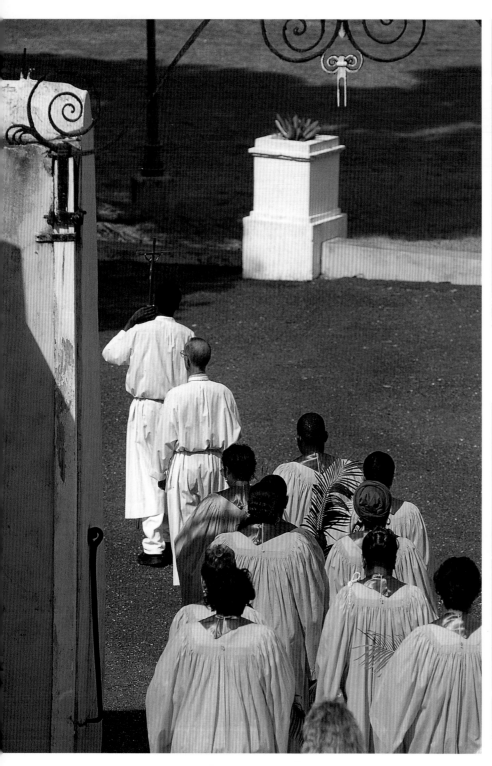

(previous page)

Buck Island

Buck Island is part of the National Park system. Located just north of St. Croix, it has been a favorite daysail destination for almost fifty years. Buck Island is a fantasy fulfilled. This stunning shot captures the bliss of water immersed in sunshine.

(above)

Palm Sunday

A procession of worshippers on Palm Sunday.

Sandy Point Wildlife Refuge

This path to the Sandy Point Wildlife Refuge ends at a broad stretch of beach where sea turtles come to lay their eggs. Active conservation measures seem to be making a difference but the future remains tenuous.

(above)

Fort Christiansvaern

The Danes had a gift for building handsome forts. Here the cannons of Fort Christiansvaern stand smartly at the ready to repel the foe—which sometimes meant the Crucian people up in arms to demand their freedom.

(left)

Church in Christiansted

More fine Danish architecture.

(opposite)

Fort Frederick

Fort Frederick presides over the roadstead of Fredericksted on the west coast of St. Croix. The wooden wheeled cannon carriage reminds visitors of the days gone by, days of slow matches and ball shot, gaff spankers and flying jibs.

(above)

Taking In the Sights

One of the most charming places to stay on St. Croix isn't on St. Croix at all, but on a small island in the middle of the Christiansted harbor, home of the Hotel on the Cay. This couple basks on its little beach, enjoying the picturesque town, yet isolated from it—until they hop the shuttle over to immerse themselves in shopping, restaurants, music and dancing.

(opposite)

Clocktower

The clocktower in downtown Christiansted.

The Pink Fancy Hotel in down-town Christiansted. Note typical arches that provided shelter from sun and rain for people on the walkways.

Island Details

Traditional wood frame house, in downtown Christiansted.

Mill at Whim, St Croix

The stone towers that dot the Crucian countryside all used to bear the windmill blades that turned the rollers that ground the cane that produced the juice that copper boilers refined into muscovado (brown sugar). When there was no wind to turn the windmill, draft animals were set to work on the animal mill.

(opposite)

Whim Plantation

The Estate Whim Plantation in St. Croix has been preserved as a museum illustrating 18th-century sugar manufacturing. The grounds and buildings are peaceful and lovely.

(above)

Cruzan Rum Distillery

The Roots of Rum. Old sugar mills like this one at the Cruzan Rum Distillery in St. Croix were used to press the juice out of sugar cane—the first operation in the process of rum production. Today Cruzan Rum is probably the Virgin Islands' best known export.

(left)

Covered Walkways

The covered walkways with their stone arches and flagstone floors are a part of Christiansted's colonial heritage.

Teague Bay
Sunrise over Teague Bay near the yacht club.

Twilight Stroll

Horse and rider pause at sunset, absorbing serenity from nature's great reserves.

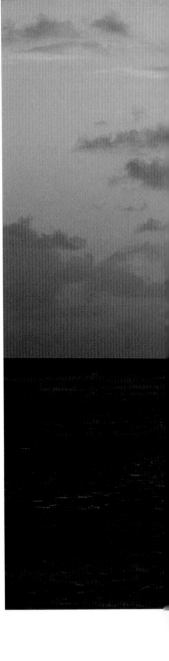

(top and bottom)

Government House

The Government House on King Street boasts a highly polished wooden ballroom floor that reflects lights like a mirror.

Cormorant Beach

Probably nothing so symbolizes the tropics, the dream of escape from the strictures and climatures of western society, as does the palm tree.

(above)

Cormorant Palms

Palm trees grow best on a beach. They provide shade, offer food and drink for the taking, and can even be fermented.

(left)

The Divi Carina Bay Casino

The Divi Carina Bay Casino is one of the most recent additions to St. Croix's architectural heritage.

(opposite)

Moonlit Cormorant Beach

One of the world's great romantic images is a full moon, a deserted beach, and a tall coconut palm rustling in the night breeze.

Zen and the Art of Casting a Fry Net

Fry is an old term for the tiny minnows that school in the hundreds of thousands (hence "small fry"). They make great bait and are best caught by throwing a round, fine meshed net made for the purpose.

Lindquist Beach

Taking time to sit and think is an
essential part of every visit.

Salt River Canyon

Salt River Canyon provides the best anchorage on St. Croix, although that didn't prevent Hurricane Hugo's gusts from tossing a trimaran 50 feet in the air at the end of its long anchor line. Columbus was believed to have stopped here on his second voyage and fought with Indians— probably Caribs—who shot off arrows while swimming, making quite an impression on the European sailors, most of whom couldn't swim at all.

(above)

Nature Conservancy, Isaac's Bay

Hardy grass and a lone cactus catch the morning light at Isaac's Bay, in St. Croix.

(left)

Rust Op Twist

In this photo Rust Op Twist appears to be a house on the prairie with clouds rolling in, but in actuality, is a restored sugar plantation (note the sugar mill to the left of the picture) and is well worth a visit.

Mirrored Palms

Palm trees on the golf course of the Buccaneer Hotel are reflected in a water trap.

Steam Engine near Cane Bay

In the later days of sugar cultivation, steam replaced wind as the power source for grinding the cane. Above is a crosshead reciprocating steam engine with its great cast iron flywheel. Similar flywheels can be found at Reef Bay and Adrian on St. John.

(above and right)

Lawaetz Museum

This classic West Indian great house dates back to the mid-1700s. The Lawaetz family lived in it until 1989, when Hurricane Hugo took off three quarters of the roof. The oldest quarter remained. After being restored, the house was turned into a museum, full of period pieces— admission free for locals on Saturday.

This beautiful bedroom in the Lawaetz Museum features a lace trimmed canopy, fine mesh mosquito net and four poster original mahogany bed. Sleeping in such a bed with the window open and a cool breeze wafting in, tinged with salt tang and night blooming cereus... such a bed should be rented out for wedding nights and honeymoons.

ST. THOMAS

(previous page)

Magens Bay

Magens Bay on a calm day shows why it is the premiere beach of the United States Virgin Islands.

(opposite)

Wooden Boat

This style of double ended wooden fishing boat is traditional to Becqia and St. Vincent in the Windward Islands, but when it comes to boats, St. Thomas sees it all.

(above)

Beached

These small fishing boats drawn up on Lindquist Bay beach are well positioned to work the cays that almost form a land bridge to St. John—Thatch, Grass, Mingo, Congo, Lovango. Note the seine net used for catching schools of bonito or blue runner.

(above)

Botany Bay

The western tip of St. Thomas is outlined in heavy surf from northerly "ground seas." These are generated by distant North Atlantic storms (November to April) and have (rarely) attained up to 20 ft in height.

(opposite)

Sapphire

The beach at Sapphire rimmed by a turquoise sea under a cobalt sky.

The Norway

The world's largest cruise ship, the Norway, draws too much water to enter the harbor. She anchors just off the south entrance and ferries her passengers ashore by tender. This magnificent vessel also stops at St. John for the best of two worlds.

Pillsbury Sound

*Cruise ship Norway entering
Pillsbury Sound.*

(above)

The Crystal Palace Guesthouse

(left)

Drake's Seat

This bench overlooking spectacular vistas on St. Thomas' north coast is supposedly where Sir Francis Drake sat on one of his visits here. The then uninhabited Virgins made a good staging area for assaults on the Spanish held islands of Puerto Rico and Santo Domingo, but the phenomenally successful English corsair failed in his attempt to take San Juan.

Sapphire Beach Resort

The Sapphire Beach Resort at the eastern tip of St. Thomas enjoys breezes right off the sea as well as a view of the islands all the way to Great Thatch and Tortola

(above)

Charlotte Amalie

A view of Charlotte Amalie from the southeast. Only the central part of the harbor is visible. Hassel Island, the green strip to the left, blocks the western arm of the bay. The eastern part, where the cruise ships dock, is behind the coconut palms.

(opposite)

Fort Christian

The red fort in the heart of town is one of the oldest and most distinctive buildings on St. Thomas. It houses the St. Thomas jail.

CURATORS
OFFICE

Legislature Building

*Bismark the great German states-
man said, "Two things men should
never see being made—laws and
sausage!" Never truer than here
and now.*

Taking Off in Charlotte Amalie Harbor

Seaplanes have linked the islands since Charlie Blair, WWII ace, started up service with a fleet of old Grumman Gooses. Those colorful, wildly romantic air-vessels roared in and out of the islands' harbors for years until, unable to get proper parts, one after another crashed. When Charlie Blair himself fatally crashed off French Cap, it was the end of an era. Today's seaplanes are newer and more reliable.

(above)

Bolongo Bay Hotel

One thing St. Thomas has is hotels. Take your pick of beaches and pools. Here palms frame a cabana and beach chairs at the Bolongo Bay Hotel.

(left)

Carnival Reveler

A beautiful reveler in full, vibrant color.

(opposite)

West End

The west end of St. Thomas still looks like a national park, with no development in sight.

Donkey at Magens Bay Overlook

Here is one who, win or lose, would happily "eat his hat". Unfortunately, wild donkeys aren't wild enough—they enjoy eating out of well kept gardens and, when desperate, can kick down substantial fences. This one earns his keep as a tourist attraction at the Magens Bay overlook.

Charlotte Amalie Alley

Alleys like this one, built of one way (outward bound) ballast bricks, run between the stately old warehouses that line the waterfront of Charlotte Amalie. One such alley, Creque's Alley, was the name of a song by the Mamas and the Papas who played a season in St. Thomas before they hit the big time.

(opposite)

99 Steps

The famous 99 steps, a shortcut built in Danish times that leads from the heart of downtown Charlotte Amalie up to Hotel 1829.

Carnival Music

Years of practice make this happy, dancy music seem easy to play.

Mocko Jumbi

Dancing tirelessly on long stilts and in brilliant flowing garb, the Mocko Jumbi is the symbol of the Virgin Islands carnival.

(opposite)

Recycling at its Creative Best!

Steel pans (drums) originated in Trinidad using discarded oil barrels. A whole musical form developed almost overnight, swept the Caribbean and became one of its proud symbols. In a steel pan orchestra everyone is a drummer.

Lobster Claw

This bright bloom native to tropical jungles is appropriately called "lobster claw."

(opposite, top)

Rennaissence Beach Resort

The beach at the Rennaissence Beach Resort.

(opposite, bottom)

Magens Bay

Magens Bay is to St. Thomas what Trunk Bay is to St. John— a surpassingly beautiful natural treasure—a bay and beach that are a landmark and totem of the island.

Mangrove Lagoons

*St. Thomas' extensive mangrove
lagoons provide a sanctuary for
juvenile fish and a great kayaking
venue, as well as protection for
boats during hurricanes.*

Simply Beautiful

This picture is like a Tarot card. The shaded fence in the foreground turns and brightens, comes to a simple, small, but beautiful house, a portal to the green sea beyond... Jung would have liked this shot.

Coki Beach and Coral World

Two of St. Thomas' favorite defining places, Coki Beach and Coral World, are just off the main road in busy Smith Bay. Coki is a beautiful beach with unusually clear water, while Coral World is a world-class seaquarium. Near each other, both can be visited on one outing.

(right)

The Marriot Frenchman's Reef

The Marriot Frenchman's Reef provides an inviting atmosphere for an evening swim.

(opposite)

The Ritz Carlton

The stunning pool at the Ritz Carlton Hotel.

(above)

Red Roof

This composition, of a traditional West Indian house, hints at the beauty of an almost vanished way of life. Note the typical louvered windows, hurricane shutters, red galvanize roof, and the abundant flowers.

Charlotte Amalie Harbor

Charlotte Amalie has one of the finest natural harbors in the West Indies—and one of the most scenic. That asset has made St. Thomas a shipping center for over three centuries. Today its sophisticated facilities and amenities make it the number one destination for cruise ships.

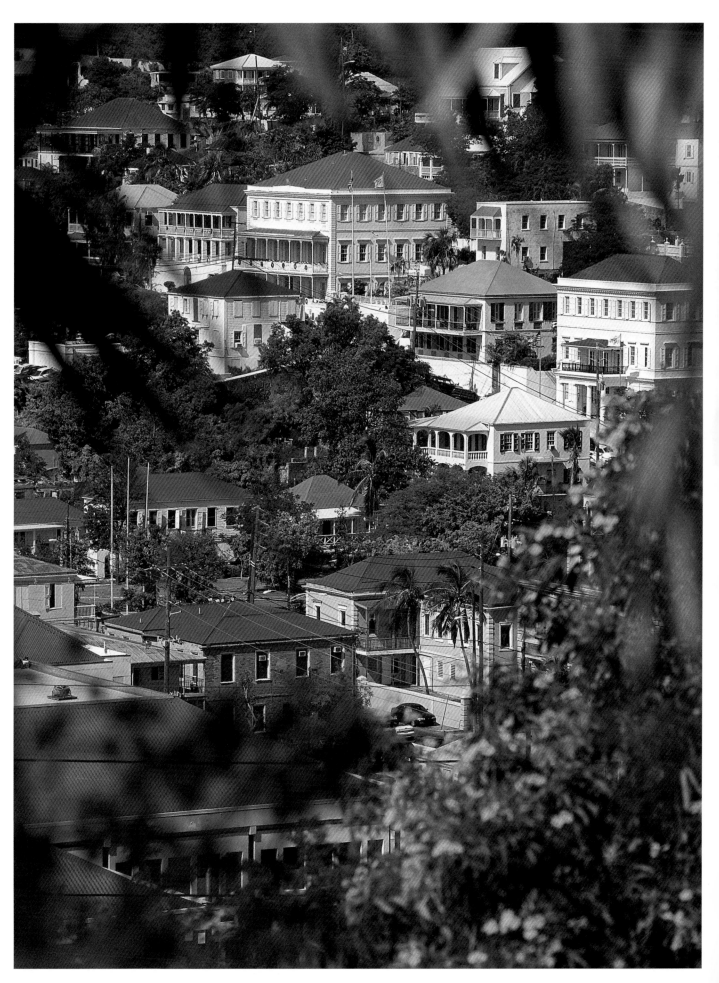

(above)

Lights of Charlotte Amalie

Lights of Charlotte Amalie and cruise ships by night from Paradise Point.

(right)

Blackbeard's Tower

Local legend has it that the famous pirate Blackbeard made St. Thomas his hangout. In those days St. Thomas thrived as a fence-cum-money laundry. Any ship was welcome to sell its cargo—no questions asked. Yo ho ho!

(opposite)

Government Hill

This lovely shot of Government Hill illustrates the interplay of attractive traditional architecture amidst hillsides and gardens that gives Charlotte Amalie its great charm.

Arwen II

A graceful ketch lies peaceably at anchor, ready for the rising sun and wind and what they might bring.

Sailboats at Redhook

Situated at the east end of St. Thomas, Red Hook marks the jumping-off point for St. John and the British Virgins. These boats are ready to raise their sails, catch the breeze and leave civilization behind.

(above)

Longspined Squirrelfish

A school of longspined squirrelfish add color and vibrance to the islands' undersea life.

(left)

Green Heron

This superbly detailed portrait of single-mindedness, a green heron intent on breakfast, belongs in the Audubon Hall of Fame—if there is one.

(opposite)

Chromis and Basslets at Little St. James

Peering into the world beneath the sea, the other senses stop as beauty explodes into the brain through the eyes.

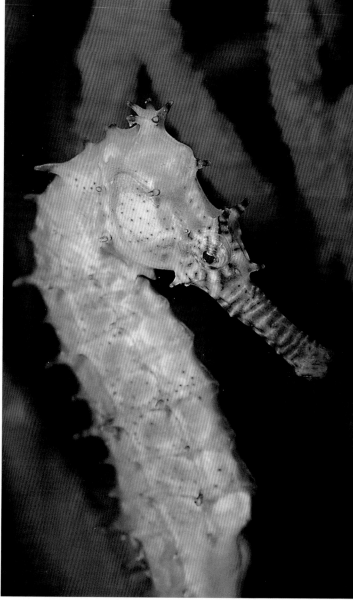

Snorkeling

The photographer's wife, looking in through the porthole of the wreck "Major General Rogers." A number of wrecks in USVI waters offer shelter to a rich array of fish and coral.

Undersea Life

Above, a seahorse poses against an orange coral backdrop. Opposite, orange crinoids with hard and soft corals.

(above)

Colors of the Deep

Above, a Queen Angelfish boasts neon blues and yellows, while a colorful reef (opposite) dances with life.